AI in HR

Enhancing Talent Acquisition and Employee Satisfaction

Table of Contents

Chapter 1. Introduction

Unravel the mystique and complexity of AI in HR with our Special Report: "AI in HR: Enhancing Talent Acquisition and Employee Satisfaction". This report provides a practical and accessible exploration of AI application in critical Human Resources functions. From talent acquisition to magnifying employee satisfaction, our comprehensive analysis navigates through the often confusing lingo and intricate technologies, breaking them down to plain-speak, everyday applications, and transformative results in the HR arena. Dissecting these advanced techniques needn't be daunting, let us be your guide in paving a clearer, potent pathway into the future of HR. Illuminate your workplace with the insights from our report so you can leverage these next-generation tools to bring about substantive improvements. You do not want to miss these transformative insights, get your copy today!

Chapter 2. Introduction to AI in HR

In recent years, the domain of human resources has undergone a dramatic transformation, primarily incited by technological breakthroughs like artificial intelligence. The advent of AI as a potent tool in the HR world has opened avenues to streamline and enhance various HR functions, leading to an improved work environment, better talent acquisition strategies, and higher employee satisfaction.

2.1. What is AI?

Artificial Intelligence, or AI, refers to the proposition of machines mimicking intelligent human behavior. It constitutes technologies capable of learning from experience, adjusting to new inputs, and performing tasks that usually necessitate human intelligence. These tasks could include interpreting natural language, identifying patterns, solving problems, and making decisions.

AI is broadly categorized into two types: Narrow AI, designed to perform a specific task such as voice recognition, and General AI, systems that can conduct any intellectual task that a human being can do. Thus far, Narrow AI is what we encounter in our everyday lives, while General AI remains largely hypothetical.

2.2. Emergence of AI in HR

Artificial intelligence in Human Resources isn't a novel idea; however, its application has amplified considerably in recent times. Initially, AI was leveraged for certain HR functions like payroll automation and record maintenance. However, continual advancements in AI technologies have unlocked its potential to revolutionize traditional HR practices, from talent acquisition to employee satisfaction.

The concept of machine learning, a subset of AI, has been integral to these developments. Machine learning algorithms use statistical techniques to give computers the ability to 'learn' from data and improve performance without being explicitly programmed to do so. Machine learning's ability to analyze vast amounts of data at breakneck speed makes it an invaluable tool in HR's arsenal.

2.3. AI in Talent Acquisition

Finding prospective employees, evaluating their suitability for a role, and on-boarding them efficiently are crucial components of any HR department's responsibilities. It's no secret that these processes, if done manually, can be time-consuming and prone to bias and errors.

With AI, the recruitment process can be optimized to provide better results. The use of Applicant Tracking Systems (ATS) that incorporate AI can filter through resumes, identifying prominent trends and red flags that may escape human notice. Moreover, AI power chatbots are being utilized for initial communication with candidates, while virtual reality and AI have found applications in employee skill assessment.

Predictive analytics, a form of AI, can be employed to ascertain the likelihood of a candidate's success in a specified role, thereby enhancing recruitment efficiency. Using AI for talent acquisition is a promising avenue, providing a more systematic, unbiased, and efficient model of recruitment.

2.4. AI in Enhancing Employee Satisfaction

Artificial intelligence also plays a significant role in improving employee satisfaction within a company. It can simplify tedious tasks, freeing employees to focus on more impactful work, thereby enhancing job satisfaction and productivity.

AI can be leveraged to provide personalized training and developmental programs utilizing training platforms that customize content based on an employee's skills, learning patterns, and career trajectory.

Moreover, AI and data analytics can be used to keep a check on employee wellbeing by analyzing patterns in an employee's communication, work patterns, and feedback, thereby identifying burnout signs and providing interventions accordingly.

The future of HR, aided by artificial intelligence, looks promising. While machines can never replace the human touch essential in HR, AI can undoubtedly be utilized as a powerful tool to streamline HR practices. By embracing AI, companies can stimulate efficiency, improve decision-making, create a conducive work environment, and above all, make their organizations future-ready.

AI doesn't come without its challenges, including ethical considerations about data privacy and the potential for bias in AI decision-making. However, with careful management and an understanding of these issues, AI can act as a robust asset in the HR portfolio.

As we venture further into the future and continue to uncover AI's full potential, it's crucial that HR professionals stay abreast of the latest developments. Stagnancy, in this age, is akin to moving backward; agility is the need of the hour. As such, this report aims to be a comprehensive guide in your journey, adequately illuminating the path towards a more effective, AI-assisted HR landscape.

Chapter 3. The Impact of AI on Talent Acquisition

Artificial intelligence (AI) is revolutionizing talent acquisition in unparalleled ways, helping HR professionals refine their practices and deliver more strategic value by streamlining repetitive tasks, minimizing human error, and supplementing decision-making with data-driven insights.

3.1. Traditional vs. AI-powered Talent Acquisition

Historically, talent acquisition encompassed arduous, time-consuming processes that were often prone to human bias and error. Recruiters would sift through hundreds, sometimes thousands, of resumes and conduct manual phone screenings to determine if a candidate met the job's basic qualifications. Many eligible candidates were overlooked, and those that were selected weren't necessarily the best-suited for the role due to these inherent limitations.

AI, however, has streamlined and enhanced these processes. It leverages machine learning algorithms to filter through resumes accurately and efficiently, pinpointing necessary skills, experiences, and qualifications. Furthermore, AI minimizes human biases by relying on data instead of emotions or subconscious prejudices, resulting in better candidate selection.

3.2. Screening and Shortlisting

AI tools can automate the initial screening phase using predefined criteria and filters. These tools parse resumes and application forms, screen candidates for qualifications and keywords, and can even assess a candidate's cultural compatibility based on predefined criteria.

AI chatbots can conduct preliminary interviews, where they can ask screening questions, answer candidate queries, and gauge interest levels. Natural language processing (NLP) and sentiment analysis techniques are frequently utilized to extrapolate added insights from these interactions.

With these technologies, HR teams can shortlist candidates who are most suited to fulfill the job requirements and align with the company culture, accelerating the pace of the recruitment process, and reducing unintentional bias.

3.3. AI in Interviews and Assessments

AI-powered interviewing platforms emulate the experience of a face-to-face interview, making remote hiring seamless. Video interviewing platforms utilize AI to assess verbal and non-verbal cues, like tone, facial expressions, word choice and speech flow.

Assessment tools leverage AI to measure candidate competencies through automated simulations, and games designed to test specific skills like problem-solving, attentiveness, and more.

The insights generated from these AI solutions provide a more comprehensive picture of candidates and ensure that recruiters can make informed decisions.

3.4. Predictive Analytics in Recruitment

Predictive analytics uses historical data and AI to predict future outcomes. In recruitment, it may predict the likelihood of a candidate accepting a job offer, their potential performance, or how well they would fit with the company culture.

By employing predictive analytics, companies can reduce attrition rates, improve productivity, and foster a more harmonious workplace environment.

3.5. Enhancing Candidate Experience

A positive candidate experience is vital to attract and retain top talent, and AI plays a pivotal role. AI chatbots provide real-time status updates, answer candidate inquiries promptly, and gather feedback post-interview.

These AI-driven practices keep candidates informed; increase transparency, engagement, and satisfaction; and strengthen the employer brand.

3.6. Bias and Discrimination in AI

Despite numerous advantages, AI isn't without its limitations. Algorithms can inadvertently amplify biases present in the historical data they're trained on. It's crucial to ensure ethical AI practices, regularly examining and refining algorithms to minimize inadvertent biases.

3.7. Conclusion

Incorporating AI in talent acquisition is no longer a luxury; it's a requirement for companies striving for efficiency, diversity, and competitiveness. AI-enhanced recruitment processes increase the speed and quality of hire, enhance candidate experience, and expedite decision-making, thereby transforming talent acquisition in profound and enduring ways. Of course, this requires constant learning, tweaking and upgrading as AI technology rapidly evolves. The future where humans and AI cooperate in talent acquisition is not only impending but is already here.

While this report provides an in-depth analysis of AI's vast impact in talent acquisition, it's crucial to remember that AI should complement human intuition and experience, not replace it. AI can handle a multitude of tasks swiftly and accurately, but the human touch, empathy, and subjective judgment are irreplaceable in recruitment. To maximize benefits, companies must find a balanced blend of AI technology and human expertise, combining high-tech with high-touch.

Remember, it's not about AI versus humans in talent acquisition; it's about AI for humans. The HR professionals who adapt to this transformation and leverage the potential of AI will undoubtedly lead the future of talent acquisition.

Chapter 4. Revamping Recruitment: AI in Resume Screening

In the world of HR, the recruitment function has seen an influx of AI applications. One of the most sought-after capabilities comes in the form of smart screening tools that can review resumes and profiles with a speed and precision unattainable by human hands. These AI-driven mechanisms have the potential to transform the way organizations attract, select, and onboard new talent.

4.1. The Basics of AI in Resume Screening

At its core, AI in resume screening works on the principles of Machine Learning (ML). It learns from existing data—derived from thousands of resumes and job profiles—about what characterizes a suitable candidate. Thereafter, the AI platform uses this learning to rank candidates for a new job role.

The idea is straightforward. You feed the AI with data—your candidate resumes—and it returns an ordered list of candidates ranked by suitability for a specific job role. But the "magic" lies beneath the surface in complex algorithms and Machine Learning models that intelligently parse through data, identify patterns, and derive insights.

4.2. Bridging the Gap: From Human Screening to AI

Historically, the task of resume screening was a manual, often tedious, process. HR recruiters spent a significant proportion of their time reading through countless CVs, recognizing that many applications received would not meet the basic entry requirements. Unfortunately, with each recruiter having a unique bias, this process lacked consistency.

Fast forward to now, ML in resume screening solves this conundrum. By use of NLP (Natural Language Processing), keyword matching, contextual understanding, and pattern recognition, resumes are shortlisted through an algorithmic process, ensuring consistency and improving efficiency.

4.3. Dissecting the Process: How AI Screens Resumes

Let's delve into the mechanics of an AI-powered resume screening tool. There are four critical stages: data input, parsing, matching, and decision making.

In the data input stage, the AI engine gathers resumes. These could be in different languages and formats. This stage also ingests the job description—the role AI will base its candidate matching on.

The parsing stage breaks down the bulk of the data. The parsing algorithm identifies specific kinds of information—contact details, educational qualifications, professional experience, skills, etc.

The matching stage comes next. Here's where the real "intelligence" comes into play. The AI solution evaluates the parsed data against the job description and key requirements of the role. Additionally, machine learning enables these AI systems to learn what an ideal candidate looks like based on previously hired candidates' data. This learning then further informs candidate ranking.

Finally, in the decision-making stage, the AI presents a graded list of candidates, ranked according to their fit for the job role.

4.4. The Impact: From Efficiency to Effectiveness

AI in resume screening has accelerated the recruitment process, ensuring efficiency and uniformity in resume evaluation. It has minimized recruiter's manual labour, mitigating 'resume fatigue', and added consistency in the screening process.

However, the efficacy of AI in recruitment is not just about speed. In addition to fast-tracking the recruitment process, AI has brought forth unprecedented levels of objectivity by eliminating human error and bias from the selection process.

4.5. Ethical Considerations: Ensuring Fairness and Reducing Bias

As we delegate decision-making to AI, it's essential to ensure these systems don't perpetuate bias. It's a valid concern as these AI models learn from historical data — data created by humans who may indeed have biases.

However, when carefully implemented, these systems can be designed to reduce bias. For instance, AI models can be trained to ignore certain information—like gender, race, or age—to ensure those factors don't impact candidate ranking.

AI in resume screening is more than a technological marvel; it's a tool that's revolutionising talent acquisition. With improved efficiency, objectivity, and fairness in resume screening, organizations are equipped better than ever to lure top-tier talent. As we continue to tread into the future, it's clear that AI's role in recruitment is only set to become more central, transformative, and indispensable.

Chapter 5. AI and Predictive Analytics in Candidate Assessment

Prediction analytics is one of the most exciting applications of Artificial Intelligence (AI) within the realm of Human Resources (HR), particularly for candidate assessment. It holds the potential not only to streamline recruitment processes but also to revamp them entirely. Predictive analytics utilizes machine learning algorithms and AI to extract information from existing data sets to identify patterns and predict future outcomes and trends.

5.1. The Fundamentals of Predictive Analytics

Predictive analytics is a form of advanced analytics that uses current and historical data to foresee future events. It combines many techniques from data mining, statistics, modeling, machine learning, and artificial intelligence to analyze present data and make forecasts about unknown future events.

In recruitment, predictive analytics can analyze historical hiring data and use machine learning algorithms to predict future hiring outcomes. This could involve predicting which candidates will perform best in a specific role, or estimating which employees are at risk of leaving. Although predictive analytics can't predict the future with absolute certainty, it can identify trends and probabilities that can significantly aid in HR decision-making.

5.2. Using Predictive Analytics for Candidate Assessment

In the context of candidate assessment, predictive analytics can be an essential tool for identifying top talent, predicting future performance, and minimizing employee turnover. By using predictive models that consider past performance and multivariate analyses of likely behavior, organizations can make more informed hiring decisions.

For instance, predictive analytics can determine which candidates are most likely to stay with the organization long-term by analyzing factors associated with employee turnover in past data. Specific information such as past job duration, reasons for leaving previous jobs, and details about career progression can all be taken into account.

Moreover, there's potential to leverage this tool to predict the performance of candidates. By modeling the characteristics of top-performing employees, predictive analytics can help to pinpoint applicants who show similar traits.

5.3. The Impact of AI in Predictive Analytics

AI plays a significant role in enhancing predictive analytics. Machine learning algorithms can read and learn from the data, getting better at predictions over time. The AI can recognize complex patterns that would go unnoticed in manual data analysis, adding a layer of intelligence to predictive analytics that makes it a potent tool for HR.

Furthermore, AI can reduce the time spent on data processing by automating the analysis and prediction processes. It can make sense of vast datasets in seconds, delivering timely predictions and insights that can guide HR decision-making.

5.4. Case Studies of Predictive Analytics in Candidate Assessment

It would be helpful to consider some case studies to demonstrate the positive impact of predictive analytics in candidate assessment.

An excellent example of a company using predictive analytics for candidate assessment is Google. They apply predictive analytics in their recruitment process to find employees who will fit well within their company culture. Google's machine-learning algorithms analyze an array of factors, including biographical information and behavioral attributes, to predict which candidates are likely to succeed within the company.

There's also the case of Marriott International, who use predictive analytics to enhance their candidate assessment. By using AI, they're able to analyze thousands of applications and predict which candidates are most likely to succeed in their organization.

Predictive analytics in candidate assessment is rapidly growing in popularity and should be given serious consideration by any forward-thinking HR department.

5.5. Implementing Predictive Analytics: Considerations and Best Practices

When implementing predictive analytics in HR, understanding the limitations and ethical implications is vital. It's essential to ensure data privacy and avoid any potential bias, which could easily creep into predictive models.

Similarly, it's crucial to remember that predictive analytics should only ever serve as a guide in decision-making. While it can help inform decisions, human intuition and expertise should still play a critical role in HR processes.

Proper data management is yet another critical aspect. Regularly testing, cleaning, and updating the data can vastly improve the accuracy of predictions.

In conclusion, predictive analytics represents a significant leap forward in the process of candidate assessment. By harnessing the full potential of AI and predictive analytics, companies can make more informed hiring decisions, resulting in improved employee satisfaction and potentially significant cost savings in the long term.

Chapter 6. Innovations in AI for Onboarding and Training

Human resources (HR) is seeing a transformation with the advent of Artificial Intelligence (AI) across its various functions. One such function is onboarding and training, where AI has begun to play a key role in revamping existing practices, leading to significant improvements in efficiency, customization, and overall employee experience.

6.1. The AI Revolution in Onboarding

HR leaders know that a well-conducted onboarding process can greatly impact a new employee's productivity, satisfaction, and long-term retention. AI has found its rightful place in this process, driving substantial enhancements.

AI-powered chatbots, for example, are transforming employee onboarding by providing interactive and personalized experiences. Unlike traditional methods involving loads of paperwork and one-size-fits-all orientation sessions, these AI bots provide new hires with role-specific information, immediate responses to queries, and a range of resources to aid the assimilation process.

AI also offers predictive analytics that can enhance the onboarding process. By identifying patterns and trends from historical data, these tools can predict what resources, information, or support a new employee might need and when. This application of AI can turn reactive onboarding into proactive platforms that adapt based on individual needs.

6.2. Leveraging AI in Employee Training

Just as with onboarding, AI is revolutionizing employee training. AI-driven training modules allow organizations to personalize learning for each employee, considering their unique learning style, knowledge level, and role requirements.

These AI systems even identify gaps in an employee's skills or knowledge, recommending targeted training programs accordingly. Such precision in identifying learning needs ensures that employees only undergo relevant training, saving valuable time and resources.

AI also comes with advanced analytics. These capabilities provide HR teams with insights like an employee's progress through a program, their strengths and weaknesses, and even the effectiveness of the training module itself. Such data-driven insights allow refinements in the training methodology, making it more effective and efficient.

6.3. Innovations in AI for Onboarding and Training

Several companies offer innovative AI solutions targeted at improving onboarding and training. For instance, Talla presents an AI-driven onboarding assistant, which uses machine learning to auto-generate personalized onboarding plans, complete with tasks and goals for the new hire. This significantly cuts down the time HR personnel would spend on these duties.

Similarly, companies like Docebo leverage AI in their learning management systems to curate personalized learning paths for each employee. Docebo's AI even offers emotion-based content delivery. This approach gauges an employee's emotional response to the content and adjusts delivery to maximize engagement and learning.

6.4. Challenges and Future Directions

While AI has opened up unprecedented opportunities, it's not without its challenges. Data privacy and security are major concerns, especially when sensitive HR data is involved. Adapting to new technology also requires a mindset change from not just HR teams but also employees. Sufficient investments in change management therefore become crucial to successful AI adoption.

But with expanding AI capabilities, its role in onboarding and training is only expected to grow. Emerging technologies like Augmented Reality (AR) and Virtual Reality (VR) present exciting possibilities when combined with AI. Imagine an onboarding experience where a new hire, through AR or VR, gets a virtual tour of the organization, or a training session where they can virtually perform their tasks.

In summary, AI has immense potential to transform HR onboarding and training. As the technology evolves and companies become more attuned to the benefits of AI, what we're witnessing now may just be the tip of the iceberg. HR leaders keen on making a significant impact in their organizations should look at AI not as an option, but a necessity.

Chapter 7. Enhancing Employee Engagement and Satisfaction with AI

Employee engagement and satisfaction are critically important elements for any organization. These parameters are a reflection of the happiness, work fulfillment, and motivated mindset of the employees, ultimately contributing to an organization's overall productivity and success. The advent of Artificial Intelligence (AI) has revolutionized the way organizations manage and enhance their employee engagement and satisfaction. AI's capability to handle large-scale data, automation, human-like interactions, real-time analysis, and predictive modeling has helped Human Resources (HR) to evolve into a more effective and strategic function.

7.1. The Birth of AI in Employee Engagement and Satisfaction

The concept of using AI in HR is no longer an alien prospect. Primarily, HR professionals are leveraging AI to simplify their tasks by automating repetitive transactional tasks, manage large-scale employee-related data, and offer personalized employee experience. From onboarding, training, feedback, motivation, to off-boarding, AI is increasingly making its presence felt in every aspect of employee lifecycle management.

Software like chatbots, intelligent virtual assistants, machine learning algorithms, and computer vision techniques are pushing the boundaries of employee engagement and satisfaction. They are enhancing transparency, personalization, and efficiency in HR processes that directly impact engagement and satisfaction levels.

7.2. The Enabler: AI in Enhancing Employee Engagement

AI has emerged as an enabler of employee engagement. It is turning HR into a more analytical function, focusing on the individual experience. AI-tools analyze data, track performance, identify skill gaps, recommend training, initiate conversations, answer queries, and provide data-driven insights for personalized engagement strategies.

AI-backed engagement platforms can send out automated surveys for real-time feedback while also conducting sentiment analysis to understand employee emotions. Tools equipped with machine learning capabilities recognize and understand an employee's intrinsic and extrinsic motivations, creating a personalized engagement program accordingly.

Moreover, AI is reducing bias and promoting growth by returning objective analyses of performance, thereby propelling a fair and balanced work ecosystem.

7.3. The Comforter: AI in Heightening Employee Satisfaction

AI's role as a comforter in enhancing employee satisfaction mirrors its abdication in fostering engagement. By automating mundane tasks and provisioning speedy service, AI helps free up an HR professional's time, enabling them to focus more on strategic decision-making.

AI-powered chatbots can handle a variety of tasks such as answering policy-related queries, assistance with leave applications, salary slips, reimbursements, or training programs, thereby ensuring speedy responses.

AI, with its predictive analysis, helps HR departments in understanding employee needs even before it has been communicated and thereby, create an environment conducive to employee satisfaction.

Furthermore, AI is utilized in creating a safe and secure workplace. Machine learning algorithms can analyze employee complaints, grievances, and feedback, helping HR to identify patterns and trends that may point toward issues like harassment or unequal treatment.

7.4. The Case Studies: Real-World Applications of AI in Engagement and Satisfaction

From global corporations to ambitious startups, organizations are using AI to enhance employee engagement and satisfaction. Here are a few case studies illustrating the beneficial impact of AI in this arena.

*IBM, through its AI platform 'Watson', is making progress in transforming its global HR function. Watson analyzes employees' skills and career aspirations and feeds them open roles and learning suggestions. It is said to have contributed effectively to their inclusive and engaging work environment.

*NextJump is another example where AI is utilized to enhance employee engagement and satisfaction levels. The company uses an AI-backed platform, which measures employees' stress levels and suggests exercises to destress and boost work productivity.

The above examples clearly illustrate how AI is bringing transformative changes in employee engagement and satisfaction.

In conclusion, the advent of AI in HR has revolutionalized not only the role of HR but the entire ecosystem of an organization. It is proven to be a catalyst, enabling organizations to enhance employee engagement and satisfaction levels to immense heights. As more companies catch on to these benefits, AI is set be the harbinger of a new era in HR.

Chapter 8. Performance Evaluation and Succession Planning through AI

The idea of incorporating Artificial Intelligence (AI) into performance evaluation and succession planning has opened up a revolutionary route in human resources (HR) management. With the advent of AI, we are shifting away from conventional manual methods towards a more systematic, unbiased, and data-driven approach. Let's delve into the intricacies of this fascinating integration to understand its contribution and effectiveness better.

8.1. The Role of AI in Performance Evaluation

Performance evaluation has long been recognized as a key HR practice to spot employee strengths and weaknesses, as well as areas needing improvement. Simply put, it is all about assessing an employee's job performance in relation to predefined indicators. AI-driven performance evaluation tools are designed to make this process more accurate, timely, and sophisticated.

AI aids in continuous performance tracking, negating the need for an integrated, one-time annual review. Instead of waiting an entire year to gauge progress, an AI can offer real-time feedback, enabling prompt corrective actions. AI can quickly interpret an employee's job role, understand performance expectations, and provide precise suggestions for improvements.

AI tools like People Analytics and Natural Language Processing (NLP) are utilized to analyze communications, team dynamics, interaction patterns, and a myriad of employee performance parameters. These tools can sift through large volumes of data, identifying patterns that might be imperceptible to the human eye. The results of these analyses can be used to personalize employee development strategies, fostering improved productivity and engagement.

Moreover, conventional performance assessments often suffer from bias, either conscious or unconscious. AI algorithms are built to identify these biases and eliminate them from the evaluation process, providing more equitable assessments.

8.2. The Pivotal Role of AI in Succession Planning

Succession planning is a critical component of strategic HR. It's about identifying and developing potential leaders who can fill key business-critical positions in the company in the future. Traditional methods involving subjective judgment and incomplete data have made this process challenging and often inaccurate. This is where AI steps in.

AI can sift through monumental volumes of data to identify patterns across roles, behaviors, abilities, and skills. It can predict pivotal personnel gaps that may occur in the future, thus empowering HR professionals to make informed and proactive decisions.

Machine learning models can reportedly predict leadership potential with higher accuracy than human intuition. These models can be trained to assess personal traits, past performance, demonstrated behaviors, and other myriad factors, enhancing the identification of potential future leaders significantly.

In addition, just as AI aids in unbiased performance evaluation, so it does in succession planning. AI algorithms can help mitigate unconscious bias in identifying potential successors, making this process more equitable and forward-thinking.

8.3. Pioneering AI Tools in Performance Evaluation and Succession Planning

Several pioneering AI tools have broken onto the scene to facilitate performance evaluation and succession planning. Engagement Multiplier and BetterWorks are becoming widely recognized for their effectiveness in monitoring employee engagement and performance. Similarly, tools like Saba and Ultimate Software incorporate AI and machine learning capabilities to identify high-potential employees suitable for succession planning.

These AI tools, founded on analytics and predictive algorithms, are invaluable companions to HR professionals, aiding them in making accurate and strategic decisions. They enable an ongoing feedback loop between managers and employees, creating a transparent culture of learning and development.

8.4. Challenges and Mitigation Measures

Despite the numerous benefits, integrating AI into performance evaluation and succession planning is not without challenges. These include data privacy concerns, risks associated with reliance solely on machine predictions, and the requisite for technology upskilling.

Resolving these issues involves implementing stringent privacy policies and protective measures, combining AI with human judgment to minimize errors and investing in upskilling initiatives to ensure employees are ready to adopt new technologies.

Artificial Intelligence has indeed infused new vigor into performance evaluation and succession planning. In combination with human expertise, AI paves the way for a future where precision, objectivity, and proactiveness are the cornerstones of strategic human resource management. Implementing AI in these arenas encourages a culture of continuous learning, fair evaluation, and merit-based succession planning. it opens the door to an exciting new phase for HR, full of immense potential and innovative possibilities.

Chapter 9. Ethical Considerations and Risks of AI in HR

Artificial Intelligence (AI) is penetrating all realms of business, leaving no function untouched. Human Resources is no exception. With AI automating repetitive tasks, enhancing the recruitment process, and allowing for a more personalized engagement with employees, HR operations are undergoing a significant transformation. However, while its benefits are manifold, it also presents new ethical considerations and risks that organizations need to grapple with.

9.1. Ethical Considerations

When integrating AI into HR functions, there are several ethical considerations that organizations must consider. These include transparency, privacy, bias, and informed consent.

9.1.1. Transparency

Transparency is vital in AI applications, including those used in HR. AI models used in HR functions should be interpretable and understandable by human users. A lack of transparency can lead to scenarios where automated HR decisions, such as talent acquisition or promotional prospects, are viewed with suspicion and lack of trust. Ensuring explainability in AI allows stakeholders to understand and trust its decision-making process.

9.1.2. Privacy

AI systems often use large amounts of data to function effectively.

However, the need for data must be carefully balanced against individual privacy rights. Given the sensitive nature of human resources - including personal data such as health records and performance evaluations - privacy becomes a crucial concern.

When integrating AI into HR, it's therefore essential to have clear policies about what data will be collected, how it will be used, and how long it will be retained. Ensuring robust data management practices, including encryption and anonymization techniques, can safeguard individuals' information and maintain their trust in the system.

9.1.3. Bias

AI systems can potentially reproduce and amplify human bias, whether it's conscious or unconscious. If bias is present in the data AI learns from, predictions and recommendations made by the system may also be biased. This is particularly concerning in HR, where such bias can have severe implications, including discriminatory hiring practices or unfair performance evaluations.

To mitigate the risk of bias, organizations need to ensure AI systems are trained on diverse, representative data. It's also crucial to periodically audit and review AI systems for any signs of biased decision making.

9.1.4. Informed Consent

Informed consent is a central ethical issue in AI applications. Employees must be made aware of the extent to which AI is making decisions that affect them. This includes what data is being collected, how AI is using it, and what decisions are being driven by automated processes. Employees should also be given the opportunity to opt out of such AI-driven processes when feasible.

9.2. Risks of AI in HR

Creating a supportive and efficient HR function using AI comes with its own set of risks. These risks include dehumanization, security vulnerabilities, job displacement, and dependency on AI.

9.2.1. Dehumanization

One of the key concerns about AI in HR is the potential for dehumanization. The shift from human-to-human interaction to human-to-machine or machine-to-machine interaction may result in a loss of empathy and personal touch. HR functions such as personal development, grievance handling, and mentoring require human understanding and relationships, which cannot be replaced by even the most advanced AI systems.

9.2.2. Security Vulnerabilities

As with any technology, security risks exist with AI. Data breaches could lead to sensitive data being leaked or misused. Additionally, the use of AI can widen the attack surface for cyber threats.

Implementing strong cybersecurity practices, regular security audits, and an incident response strategy is essential to mitigate these risks.

9.2.3. Job Displacement

The deployment of AI will likely automate certain tasks, particularly those that are repetitive and high-volume. This could lead to job displacement in HR, raising concerns about job security.

It's crucial for organizations to manage this transition carefully. Reskilling and upskilling initiatives can help prepare employees for newer, more strategic roles where human intelligence is critical.

9.2.4. Dependency on AI

Increased efficiency and effectiveness of HR tasks through AI might create a dependency on this technology. This could prove risky if there are system failures or if the AI makes a mistake.

Therefore, HR functions should maintain a certain level of human oversight to review decisions made by AI, ensuring a blend of human judgment with AI efficiency.

In conclusion, while AI offers exciting opportunities for HR functions, these ethical considerations and risks cannot be ignored. A balanced approach is required that harnesses the power of AI while taking proactive measures to mitigate these ethical and risk concerns. Only then can AI truly uplift HR functions in a sustainable and inclusive manner.

Chapter 10. Future Trends: The AI-Driven Shift in HR

The adoption of Artificial Intelligence (AI) has been steadily gaining traction across various industries, and Human Resources (HR) is no exception. As we head deeper into the 21st century, HR functions are continually reshaped by the transformative power of AI. This AI-driven shift in HR has profound implications for the future of work, influencing how companies recruit, manage, and retain talent.

10.1. The Role of AI in Recruitment

One of the most significant trends in HR's future is the shift towards AI-powered recruitment. Recruitment is a time-consuming and costly process; AI holds the potential to streamline this with increased efficiency and accuracy. AI can significantly reduce the time to hire by streamlining candidate sourcing, resume screening, and even preliminary interviews using chatbots. This automation enables HR professionals to focus on higher-level tasks and ensures a swifter, more efficient recruitment process.

AI can also help improve the quality of hire. Machine learning algorithms can parse through resumes and job descriptions, predicting an applicants' success based on a vast array of parameters such as past employment history, education, and even keyword usage. This aids in eliminating less-qualified candidates and identifies those most likely to succeed, thereby increasing the overall quality of the new hires.

10.2. Enhancing Employee Engagement and Satisfaction Through AI

AI is not only transforming recruitment procedures but also plays a pivotal role in enhancing employee engagement and satisfaction. One of the ways this is achieved is through recommendation engines. These AI-driven systems make personalized learning and development recommendations to employees, similar to how Netflix suggests shows based on viewing history. This way, staff members feel seen and understood, leading to increased job satisfaction.

Furthermore, AI can provide real-time sentiment analysis of employee communication, providing HR departments with valuable insights into the workforce's emotional state. These insights can help companies to tackle employee dissatisfaction swiftly and prevent conflicts even before they arise.

10.3. AI for Performance Management and Succession Planning

Performance management and succession planning are traditionally HR functions that involve much subjectivity. However, AI can bring in data-powered objectivity. AI systems can continuously monitor and assess employee performance based on a multitude of parameters, providing consistent, unbiased data on each worker. Besides performance, AI can also objectively analyze an employees' potential, thereby easing succession planning.

These AI platforms give managers the tools to track, record, and analyze employees' skills, strengths, and areas of improvement. By doing so, managers have a better understanding of their team's capabilities, allowing them to manage performances more optimally. This not only improves their decision-making process but also fosters fairness and transparency, leading to improved employee morale.

10.4. AI in Workforce Planning and Predictive Analytics

In the future, AI will continue to play a significant role in workforce planning and predictive analytics. AI can help HR professionals predict future trends in the labor market, providing data-driven evidence to support strategic planning. Additionally, predictive analytics can forecast potential turnover rates, identifying periods of increased turnover risk. This ability to anticipate and plan can save companies significant resources and time.

In an increasingly competitive business environment where attracting and retaining top talent can make or break a company, these predictive capabilities of AI are invaluable, paving the way for a more proactive, rather than reactive HR approach.

10.5. The Ethical and Security Challenges of AI

While the benefits of AI in HR are apparent, future trends also indicate a need to tackle the ethical and security challenges that come with AI. From managing bias in AI algorithms to protecting employee data, HR needs to address these issues head-on to maintain trust and compliance.

HR departments must work in tandem with IT to address these challenges, ensuring that AI deployments are not only efficient and effective, but secure and ethical. This involves regular audits of AI systems, transparency in algorithm outcomes, and attention to security practices around employee data.

In conclusion, the future of HR is inexorably tied to the advancement and adaptation of AI. While the exact outcomes are unknown, one thing is certain: AI, when effectively harnessed, can create unparalleled efficiency, objectivity, and future-readiness in HR functions. As we forge ahead, the challenge lies not just in adopting these AI trends in HR, but also in overcoming their associated ethical and security challenges.

Chapter 11. Case Studies: Success Stories Harnessing AI in HR

Artificial intelligence is reshaping the face of business processes, and Human Resources is not left behind. Many companies worldwide have successfully used AI to streamline their HR processes - from recruitment to staff management and training. In this chapter, we'll look at some of these exciting case studies that serve as shining lights in the potential of AI in HR.

11.1. The IBM Watson Transformation

IBM, a frontrunner in the technological field, utilized their powerful AI, Watson, to revolutionize their HR processes. The results have been nothing short of extraordinary.

IBM implemented AI in their talent acquisition process. Initially, the process involved hours of manually filtering through thousands of resumes. With Watson, the hiring team could now automatically screen applicants based on predefined criteria. The system even enabled rank scoring to determine the most qualified candidates based on job descriptions.

A crucial feature of Watson is its natural language processing capabilities. It enabled the screening process to become more intuitive, recognizing factors such as abilities, experience, and compatibility. IBM reported significant improvements in the hiring process: applications were reviewed 66% faster, and the company could hire top talent 20% faster.

The AI advancements didn't stop at recruitment. IBM also used Watson's cognitive computing abilities to advise managers on establishing higher employee engagement and improving decision-making. Managers could ask the AI system about team data and factors affecting performance.

AI's impact on IBM's HR division was dramatic. It transformed how they attracted, hired, and retained talent, setting a new HR industry standard.

11.2. Cogito and Behavioral Adaptation

Cogito specializes in real-time emotional intelligence solutions. Its AI platform has been instrumental in enhancing customer service interactions.

In HR, Cogito's AI platform helps managers be more effective by analyzing real-time conversational dynamics and providing behavioral guidance. The tool assists in improving managers' interaction with their team members.

The AI platform offers live coaching during calls, giving instant feedback on the manager's conversational tactics. Factors like talking speed, voice volume, and listening skills are analyzed. The manager can then make instant corrections, leading to more effective communication.

Post-call analytics are also provided, giving a comprehensive breakdown of the conversation. This feedback improves future interactions, leading to increased employee satisfaction and engagement.

11.3. Hilton and the AI-powered Recruitment

Hilton, the multinational hospitality company, leveraged AI to enhance its recruitment process. The firm developed an AI-powered robot, Connie the concierge, to liaise with applicants.

Connie helps potential candidates navigate through the application process, providing feedback in real-time. Vital skills required for the job are tested during interactive sessions with the bot.

In just under a year, Connie had effectively reduced Hilton's time-to-hire by 85%. The AI system has not only made the hiring process more efficient but has also improved the candidate experience.

11.4. Uber and the Driver Satisfaction Algorithm

Uber provides an interesting case study when it comes to AI in HR. They developed an AI system to improve their drivers' satisfaction and reduce workforce turnover.

Uber's AI algorithm analyzes data points from drivers' daily routines, including rest periods, working hours, and earnings. It uses this data to provide drivers with targeted suggestions aimed at maximizing their earnings and work satisfaction.

Through the algorithm, Uber saw a noticeable improvement in driver retention rates. Drivers felt more valued, and the job became more sustainable, providing proof that AI in HR is a game-changer.

11.5. Unilever and Digital Hiring Process

Unilever, the consumer-goods giant, digitized its hiring process by leveraging AI. Their digital hiring process includes an AI-assessed video interview and games that measure a candidate's potential beyond their CV.

The system provides an analysis of a candidate's word choice, body language, and speech during the video interview. The AI applies neuro-linguistic programming, providing a more comprehensive assessment of the candidates.

Unilever reported that this hiring process strategy reduced hiring time from 4 months to four weeks. It also resulted in a happier and more engaged workforce.

These case studies represent the vast potential of AI in HR. Each case delivers a clear message – AI tools can vastly improve HR processes. Whether it's finding and attracting the right talent, improving employee engagement, or honing management skills, AI is leading the way, rewriting the HR rulebook, and propelling the HR role into an exciting future.

www.ingramcontent.com/pod-product-compliance
Lightning Source LLC
Chambersburg PA
CBHW061056050326
40690CB00012B/2639